>> CODE POWER: A TEEN PROGRAMMER'S GUIDE™

GETTING TO KNOW

JavaScript

DONNA B. MCKINNEY

rosen publishing's
**rosen
central**

New York

Published in 2019 by The Rosen Publishing Group, Inc.
29 East 21st Street, New York, NY 10010

Library of Congress Cataloging-in-Publication Data

Names: McKinney, Donna Bowen, author.
Title: Getting to know JavaScript / Donna B. McKinney.
Description: First edition. | New York : Rosen Publishing, 2019. | Series: Code power : a teen programmer's guide | Includes bibliographical references and index. | Audience: Grades 5–8.
Identifiers: LCCN 2018008362| ISBN 9781508183778 (library bound) | ISBN 9781508183754 (pbk.)
Subjects: LCSH: JavaScript (Computer program language)—Juvenile literature.
Classification: LCC QA76.73.J39 M394 2019 | DDC 005.2/762—dc23
LC record available at https://lccn.loc.gov/2018008362

Manufactured in the United States of America

{CONTENTS

P eople need a way to talk to computers. If someone learned Spanish or French or German, to name just a few human languages, he or she would be able to communicate with other people who also speak those same languages. In a similar way, people use programming languages to communicate instructions to a computer. These instructions are called programs, and they tell the computer to complete certain tasks.

There are many programming languages that people use to create software programs—the instructions that tell a computer what to do. The job of writing the programs is called programming or coding. JavaScript is just one of these computer programming languages.

Different programming languages might be used depending on the task the programmer wants a computer to perform. The computer will run whatever instructions it is given. So it is up to the programmer to choose the best language for a certain job.

Not everyone knows exactly what JavaScript is or what it does. However, anyone who has spent time browsing the internet has most likely seen what JavaScript does. If you have visited familiar social media sites like Twitter or Facebook, you have seen JavaScript at work. If you play video games, you have seen JavaScript at work there, too. If you shop on a website like

UCTION

Amazon, you have seen JavaScript in action. Programmers use JavaScript as they develop websites so users can interact with the site. JavaScript also is used to develop animations and other special effects.

While there are hundreds of programming languages available for programmers to use, any list of the most popular

>> JavaScript is just one of many programming languages available to a programmer for writing instructions that a computer will execute.

programming languages would include JavaScript. Since JavaScript can be run from almost all web browsers, it is easy to see why it is so popular. Every time a person connects to the internet from a personal computer or mobile device, JavaScript is available. Stack Overflow's 2017 developer survey documents JavaScript's popularity. In what Stack Overflow described as the "largest developer survey ever conducted," JavaScript was named the most popular computer language. "For the fifth year in a row, JavaScript was the most commonly used programming language," according to the Stack Overflow survey. RedMonk also publishes regular programming language rankings—their list included JavaScript in the number-one slot as the most popular programming language in 2017.

JavaScript is a language that continues to grow and mature as a tool for building complex programs. New JavaScript tools and libraries are always popping up in the JavaScript world, while new versions of JavaScript are being released on a regular basis.

With so many programming languages available, someone might wonder, "why learn JavaScript?" For starters, JavaScript is considered to be easier to learn than many other languages. Although JavaScript is simple enough that people who are not programmers can learn it, the language is powerful enough to be a handy part of the professional programmer's toolbox. To use JavaScript, a programmer simply inserts the code on the web page. JavaScript can be run from a web browser without the need for any additional software programs. It is a very flexible and effective language for the programmer wanting to create a website with interactive elements that function well for the user and are also appealing to the eye.

CHAPTER 1

JAVASCRIPT: IT'S A COMPUTER LANGUAGE

Before diving into the details of JavaScript—what it is, how it works, what it can do—it is helpful to lay the foundation of basic computer programming concepts.

A computer can complete many tasks, ranging from simple to highly complex. Before that computer begins any task, it needs instructions that tell it what to do. A computer program is a set of instructions that tell the computer what to do.

If only computers spoke the same languages humans do, it might be easier to communicate with them. However, a computer's language consists of 1s and 0s. So humans have developed computer languages that allow them to communicate with the machines more easily.

In the early days of computer programming, the programs were written in machine code (or machine language) and assembly language, a basic, low-level programming language. Machine code is sometimes called native code. This machine code used the computer's language of 1s and 0s. This kind of code is described as a low-level programming language.

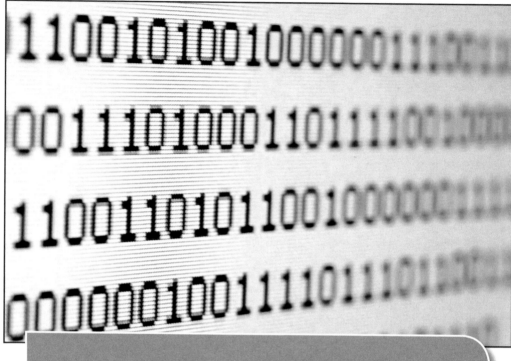

>> In simple form, computers use the language of 1s and 0s—or binary code.

TO COMPILE OR INTERPRET?

Along with the low-level languages, there are also high-level languages that are more like human languages (and less like the machine languages). Programmers generally find these high-level languages easier to read and write than the low-level languages. High-level languages are translated into machine language so that the computer can execute the commands. This is done with either a compiler or interpreter. So the programming languages can be divided into two categories: compiled languages and interpreted languages.

>>COMPUTER PROGRAMMING LANGUAGE—THEN AND NOW

A computer programming language is the coded language a programmer uses to tell the computer what to do. It can be thought of as a set of instructions, written out as a series of short, specific commands. Just like the spoken languages that humans use, every programming language has its own syntax (or grammar rules) and its own semantics (or meanings).

(continued on the next page)

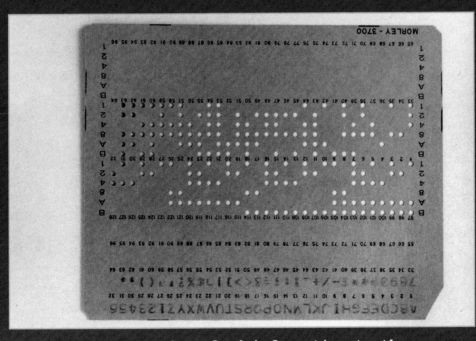

>> Programmers used to feed information to the computer using a punch card, like this, where the holes in the card represented data to be interpreted.

> *(continued from the previous page)*
>
> The earliest programming languages, created in the 1940s, were written in binary form (Os and 1s, or ON and OFF). Programmers had to move the memory in the machines by hand. This kind of programming was time consuming and difficult for humans to understand.
>
> In the 1950s, people began to create programming languages that used symbols to represent the machine-language commands. With these languages, programmers used an assembler to translate the symbols into the binary form that the computer understood. This was still a very complex way to program, and it was easy for errors to creep into the instructions.
>
> The languages programmers use today continue to evolve, making the programming easier (compared to the binary code in the earliest days of the computer) and less prone to mistakes in the coding process.

Compiled programming languages have to be run through a compiler (a software program) that translates the code a person wrote into machine code that a computer understands and can execute. The compiled languages usually run faster than the interpreted languages. Some examples of compiled languages are Ada, BASIC, C, COBOL, Fortran, and Pascal.

JAVASCRIPT—AN INTERPRETED LANGUAGE

With interpreted programming languages, the language is translated to a machine language, but the user's web browser does the translating while the program is being run. JavaScript is a high-level interpreted programming language. These languages do not have to be run through a compiler before the computer can run the program. Some other examples of interpreted languages are MATLAB, Perl, PHP, and Ruby.

One advantage to the interpreted languages is that a programmer can insert changes to the program easily, at any point. A disadvantage to the interpreted language is that because it is being translated while the program is being run, the programs tend to run a little slower. As the interpreters are becoming more efficient, the speed difference between compiled languages and interpreted languages is decreasing.

JAVASCRIPT—A CLIENT-SIDE SCRIPTING LANGUAGE

Programmers typically work with compiled languages to create software applications. They generally use the interpreted languages to run scripts—short computer

>> Web browsers like Firefox, Chrome, or Safari all provide the "engine" that runs JavaScript on so many different devices.

programs that give commands. JavaScript is a client-side scripting language. This means that the web browser (also called the client) a person uses is the engine that interprets the program and runs the scripts. This engine gives JavaScript all that it needs to operate in that browser.

Familiar web browsers include Mozilla Firefox, Google Chrome, or Apple Safari. It is possible to run JavaScript without a web browser, using just an engine. Google V8 is one example

>>PROGRAMMER, CODER, OR DEVELOPER—WHICH IS IT?

Some people use the words "programmer," "coder," or "developer" interchangeably to describe a person who writes code to create software. Other people see differences between the three words—with the job title of programmer sounding a little more professional than coder. (Some programmers might not want to be called coders.) Coders are typically considered to be the least experienced programmers. The developer and programmer job titles sometimes mean the same thing, varying from business to business. However, a developer job is often more of a generalist position and calls for a person who has programming skills along with strong people skills working in team settings—someone who oversees web development and design projects from start to finish.

of this kind of engine. Just like in car racing, where a faster engine is desirable, programmers also want faster engines for running JavaScript. Most of the current JavaScript engines use an interpreting process called Just-In-Time (JIT) that increases the speed of a program.

JAVASCRIPT SYNTAX

When learning English, children commonly learn to speak before writing. As they learn to write it, children also have to learn more of the rules that govern the language—how to arrange the words and punctuation in a way that makes sense and is grammatically correct. This is called the language's syntax. Syntax also refers to the rules of the computer languages.

> In JavaScript, tags like this are common: <**script**>.
> Symbols are also common: parentheses **( )** or semicolons **;** or brackets **{ }** or plus signs **+** or quote marks **" '**.
> Shortened words like **var** or **console.log** also appear frequently.
> The **<script>** tag is actually an HTML tag, and it tells the computer that the JavaScript instructions that follow the tag are to be executed when the web page is opened.

These syntax rules may seem confusing for a person just learning to program, but practice working with JavaScript (or any computer language) is the key. With practice comes familiarity and confidence in writing the code.

```
se c=void 0}return c}function P(a){var b;for(b in a)if(("data"!==b
ect(a[b]))&&"toJSON"!==b)return!1;return!0}function Q(a,b,d,e){if(m.
h=m.expando,i=a.nodeType,j=i?m.cache:a,k=i?a[h]:a[h]&&h;if(k&&j[k]&&
==d||"string"!=typeof b)return k||(k=i?a[h]=c.pop()||m.guid++:h),j[k
.noop}),("object"==typeof b||"function"==typeof b)&&(e?j[k]=m.extenc
tend(j[k].data,b)),g=j[k],e||(g.data||(g.data={}),g=g.data),void 0!=
b)]=d),"string"==typeof b?(f=g[b],null==f&&(f=g[m.camelCase(b)])):f=
f(m.acceptData(a)){var d,e,f=a.nodeType,g=f?m.cache:a,h=f?a[m.expan
f(b&&(d=c?g[h]:g[h].data)){m.isArray(b)?b=b.concat(m.map(b,m.camelC
m.camelCase(b),b=b in d?[b]:b.split(" ")),e=b.length;for(;e--;)dele
.isEmptyObject(d))return}(c||(delete g[h].data,P(g[h])))&&(f?m.clea
pando||g!=g.window?delete g[h]:g[h]=null)}}}function ab(){return!0}
function cb(){try{return y.activeElement}catch(a){}}function db(a){v
reateDocumentFragment();if(c.createElement)for(;b.length;)c.createl
}function ub(a,b){var c,d,e=0,f=typeof a.getElementsByTagName!==K?a
b||"*"):typeof a.querySelectorAll!==K?a.querySelectorAll(b||"*"):vc
a.childNodes||a;null!=(d=c[e]);e++)!b||m.nodeName(d,b)?f.push(d):m
void 0===b||b&&m.nodeName(a,b)?m.merge([a],f):f}function vb(a){W.tc
ecked=a.checked)}function wb(a,b){return m.nodeName(a,"table")&&m.r
b:b.firstChild,"tr")?a.getElementsByTagName("tbody")[0]||a.appendCl
t.createElement("tbody")):a}function xb(a){return a.type=(null!==m
a.type.a}function vb(a){var b=nb.exec(a.type);return b?a.type=b[1
```

While uppercase and lowercase do not always matter as much in English, JavaScript is a case-sensitive language. That means that handling uppercase and lowercase letters consistently is important in order for the computer to understand and follow the instructions the programmer is giving.

HOW JAVASCRIPT WAS BORN

n the beginning, JavaScript was called Mocha. Then it was called LiveScript. Finally, it was called JavaScript, and that name stuck. The year was 1995, and the internet was very young. Netscape Communications Corporation had developed a web browser—Netscape Navigator (later renamed Netscape Communicator)—that was growing in popularity.

Marc Andreessen, who founded Netscape Communications, was looking for ways to take advantage of the web's increasing popularity. Andreessen thought that animations and interaction would play an important role in the web as it grew. For the web to grow in these areas, Andreessen knew there needed to be a programming language that could make these things happen. This language would not be created only for use by developers, programmers, and software engineers. Andreessen wanted to create a simple scripting language that could be learned and used by nondevelopers, too, to make web applications exciting.

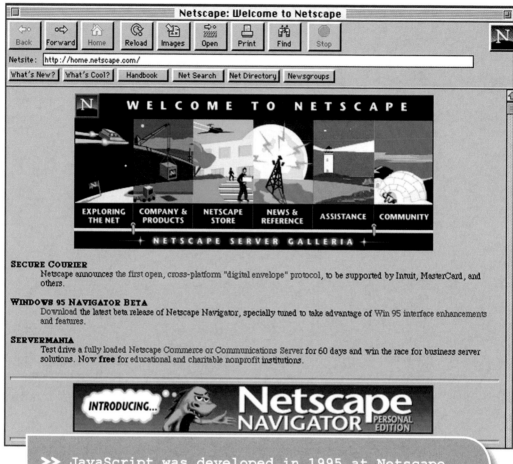

BRENDAN EICH—FATHER OF JAVASCRIPT

Netscape assigned Brendan Eich to develop this programming language for their Navigator web browser. Brendan Eich is regarded today as the father of JavaScript. They gave the project the name Mocha at the beginning. Eich explained how it started in an interview with InfoWorld, saying, "The idea was to make something that Web designers, people who may or may not have much programming training, could use to add a little bit of animation or a little bit of smarts to their Web forms and their Web pages." Eich's initial work in creating JavaScript took place from May until December 1995.

The idea behind the JavaScript name, Eich explained, was to make this new language a complimentary scripting language that worked with the programming language Java. Eich worked quickly, creating a prototype of Mocha in just a few weeks. In developing JavaScript, he borrowed elements from existing computer languages, such as AWK, Java, Self, HyperTalk, and Scheme. He had to work quickly because the competition

>> When JavaScript was developed, the programming language Java already existed—JavaScript was intended to be a scripting language that worked alongside Java.

between Netscape and Microsoft was strong at this time. (Microsoft would introduce its own version of JavaScript, called Jscript, just a year after JavaScript was launched. Jscript was part of the Internet Explorer web browser.)

JAVASCRIPT EMERGES

In May 1995, this prototype of Mocha was added to the Netscape browser. By December 1995, Netscape and Sun Microsystems joined forces in a licensing agreement and the new product was renamed JavaScript. The companies would introduce JavaScript as a scripting language for small tasks working in the browser. Java was viewed as a more professional tool, used by programmers and developers for more complex web components. This earliest version of JavaScript contained many of the functional features found in the latest version of the language. That first public release of JavaScript occurred in 1995, when it came out as part of the web browser Netscape Navigator 2.0.

From its earliest days, JavaScript was very popular. It improved the computer user's experience so that competing web browsers had to move quickly to add some form of JavaScript to their browser. Netscape and Microsoft both worked hard to add more special features to their products to gain the advantage in sales. Some people called this competition between the two companies the Browser Wars. The end result was extra work for programmers, who had to write two different versions of code for any project they worked on, so that the program would run properly in both Netscape's and Microsoft's browsers.

Over time, Microsoft's Internet Explorer captured the spot as the more dominant browser. Programmers, developers, and others in the computer industry began to call for standards to be set for JavaScript. With better standards, programmers and developers would be able to produce applications that behaved reliably on the different web browsers.

>>CODING PIONEERS

Many people have contributed to today's technology, especially related to computer programming and programming languages. Here are just a few of the coding pioneers:

Charles Babbage: A mathematician in the 1800s, he thought up the concept for a machine with an input device, a processor, a control unit, and an output device. He called it the Analytical Engine.

Ada Lovelace: A friend of Charles Babbage, she wrote the first computer program for Babbage's Analytical Engine. Lovelace is generally recognized as the world's first computer programmer.

Alan Turing: He thought up the idea for the Universal Turing Machine, a device that could be programmed to perform different tasks.

Grace Hopper: She was a US Navy officer who achieved the rank of rear admiral and created the first compiler tool, which eventually led to the development of the computer language called COBOL.

(continued on the next page)

(continued from the previous page)

John Atanasoff: He invented the first digital computer. His Atanasoff-Berry Computer was tested for the first time in 1942.

Margaret Hamilton: She led the development of the on-board flight software used to guide the Apollo spacecraft in the moon landings in the 1960s and 1970s.

Tim Berners-Lee: He is credited with inventing the World Wide Web in 1989.

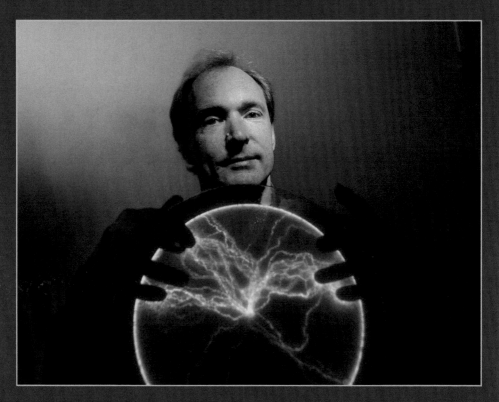

>> In 1989, Tim Berners-Lee invented the World Wide Web. He is one of the most respected computer scientists of all time.

JAVASCRIPT'S POPULARITY GROWS

JavaScript grew quickly in popularity. In a November 1996 news release issued by Netscape, JavaScript's surge in popularity is described this way:

> JavaScript and Java are cornerstone technologies of the Netscape ONE platform for developing Internet and Intranet applications. In the short time since their introduction last year, the new languages have seen rapid developer acceptance with more than 175,000 Java applets and more than 300,000 JavaScript-enabled pages on the Internet today according to www.hotbot.com. With Java and JavaScript support incorporated into both its client and server products, Netscape is the most widely deployed software platform for building and running Java based applications, with millions of users worldwide.

After that initial public release of JavaScript, the next big thing for the language was ECMA standardization. ECMA International is the European Computer Manufacturers Association. The organization formed in 1961 to create standards for computer systems. In 1996, ECMA began work on the standard for a general purpose scripting language—which describes JavaScript. When the JavaScript standard was published, it was named ECMAScript and the number was ECMA-262. (JavaScript is ECMAScript's commercial name.) ECMAScript gives the rules and guidelines that set the standard for a scripting language.

Having a standard is important because different companies make the various web browsers available to computer users. By following the ECMA standard, all browsers will execute the JavaScript code in the same way. The group that developed the standard is named Technical Committee 39 (TC-39). This group consists of representatives from the major web browser companies, including Apple, Google, Microsoft, and Mozilla, along with other members who are experienced in web development. TC-39 continues to work at maintaining and updating ECMAScript.

AJAX ARRIVES

Around 2005, the term Ajax (Asynchronous JavaScript and XML) came into use. The Ajax technique allowed the data obtained

from a server to update only the relevant parts of a web page without reloading or refreshing the whole page. This technique improves a user's web experience by making it more convenient, seamless, and efficient. Ajax is not its own programming language—it is a technique for using technologies that already exist in some more efficient ways.

>> Ajax—or Asynchronous JavaScript and XML—a useful technique that emerged around 2005, made a user's web experience more efficient and boosted JavaScript's popularity.

With the arrival of Ajax, JavaScript's popularity grew. Professional computer programmers took a fresh look at using JavaScript, and programmers began to create JavaScript libraries—where JavaScript code to perform certain tasks was shared among programmers, making everyone's job a little easier.

JavaScript has now been a part of the computer programming languages world for more than twenty years. Brendan Eich described how JavaScript has grown in popularity since he dreamed it up back in 1995. In an interview with InfoWorld, he said, "The Web is the biggest, broadest platform, maybe not the best platform … But the Web is what everybody wants to use. You get a browser and an internet kiosk, you can use it. So if JavaScript is the scripting language of the Web, it has the most reach." As JavaScript continues to change and grow to meet ever-changing technology needs, the future does look bright for this language.

CHAPTER 3

JAVASCRIPT AND WEB CONTENT

Millions of people use JavaScript every day without ever noticing it. An online form, for example, in which the user enters information and then clicks "OK" is using features enabled by JavaScript. Interactive online games use features enabled by JavaScript. JavaScript is there at work, powering the web pages of the familiar websites anyone might use. Websites like Facebook, eBay, Amazon Marketplace, Etsy, Instagram, and Gmail are just a few examples of sites with interactive features made possible by JavaScript. Programmers add JavaScript by inserting snippets of JavaScript code—these are called scripts—into the header or body of the document that becomes a web page. Here is how it works.

THREE-LAYER CAKE OF WEB TECHNOLOGIES

Programmers use JavaScript to tell the web browser what to do, but JavaScript does not work alone. There are some other important web technologies that help the web page do everything the programmer wants. Some programmers use the idea of a

>> Any time users interact with a website—eBay is just one familiar example—JavaScript is powering what happens on the web page.

three-layer cake to describe how JavaScript, HTML (Hypertext Markup Language), and CSS (Cascading Style Sheets) go together to provide users with the content updates, interactive features, and special-effect graphics seen on a web page. Each of these layers—HTML, CSS, JavaScript—serve an important function to tie the website together.

HTML is not a programming language. Instead, it is a kind of markup language that uses tags, or elements. HTML gives a website its structure. HTML defines the paragraphs, headers, tables, or embedded images on the web page. In the 1990s, the early days of the internet, HTML was the only language developers had to build web pages. Coding each page of a website was a slow, tedious process. So much has changed with respect to the tools modern programmers and developers have at hand for designing and building web pages.

HTML EXAMPLES:

Here are some common HTML tags, used to help display a header, a title, or the body text.
<head>
<title>
<body>

All HTML tags have a beginning and ending tag, as shown below:

All these words would be bold print on the web page.

<p>All these words would be a paragraph on the web page.</p>

CSS, like HTML, is not a programming language. Instead, as its name implies, it is a style sheet language. It gives a website's content its style (layout, background color,

>> CSS is a style sheet computer language that controls how a website is presented, formatted, and laid out.

fonts, and margins). CSS also allows programmers to manage the layout on a number of web pages at one time so they can save time when using CSS. Programmers use CSS to control the way the website is presented, formatted, and laid out.

Programmers can add CSS to the HTML tags in three different ways:

- Programmers add CSS inline using the style attribute in HTML tags.
- Programmers add CSS internally using a <style> tag in the <head> section of the document.
- Programmers add CSS externally using an external CSS file.

JavaScript is used alongside HTML and CSS to control how all the different parts of the web page behave. JavaScript allows the programmers to give their websites interactive features. These interactive features allow the computer user to do something, and then the website responds.

STATIC WEBSITES

In the early days of the internet, websites were static, or unchanging. They were simple, basic websites, built with HTML code. Each page was a separate HTML file, and the website consisted of this collection of files or pages. No programming was used for these pages. Think of it as appearing somewhat like a newspaper page—it looks the same every time the page is loaded.

>> The earliest websites built with HTML code, such as in this example, were simple and unchanging in appearance.

By comparison, a dynamic website appears differently depending on the user or the situation. The website can generate fresh content as needed to display different things in different circumstances. A dynamic website also uses HTML and CSS, which gives the website its structure and style. To be truly dynamic, however, a programmer must use a scripting language like JavaScript—that third layer of the cake. The programmer adds JavaScript right into the web page's HTML. With JavaScript added in, the website becomes something that people can use, not simply read. Dynamic websites work this way: when a user goes to a specific web address, the server gathers pieces of information and builds a web page that the user sees.

So without JavaScript, a web page is static and it will remain static. JavaScript code will allow a website to be more interactive, more user friendly, and more visually appealing. Users find it easier to navigate a JavaScript website. With JavaScript, programmers can automate certain features—like writing a personalized greeting to the user when he or she opens the page. JavaScript also has the capability to make these changes without reloading the whole page—thanks to Ajax. Google Maps is one familiar application that uses Ajax to change and manipulate its maps in real time, without needing to reload the page.

>>JAVASCRIPT—STRENGTHS/ WEAKNESSES

As with all programming languages, JavaScript has its strengths and weaknesses. Here are some that programmers name:

Strengths
- Internet and web browsers are familiar to most computer users—so to start using JavaScript, all someone needs to do is open a browser and begin to type code.

(continued on the next page)

(continued from the previous page)

- Compared with some other programming languages, JavaScript is simpler and easier to learn.
- JavaScript is among the most popular languages in the world.
- JavaScript is fast since the code runs from the web browser—it does not have to connect with a server and wait for a response.
- JavaScript runs from both the front end (web browser) and back end (server).
- JavaScript works alongside other languages and offers a wide range of applications.

Weaknesses
- JavaScript can be vulnerable to some security problems because it runs on the user's computer.
- Because JavaScript is single thread (i.e., executes one command at a time), some think it works more slowly.
- JavaScript can look different from one computer to the next because different browsers implement JavaScript in slightly different ways.

JAVASCRIPT OUTSIDE WEB PAGES

JavaScript was initially designed to work in a user's web browser. Working with JavaScript, programmers could write the code that tells a website how to behave. This part of the development process is called front-end development—it is the front end of the website. Then in 2009, a software engineer named Ryan Dahl invented Node.js (most people just call it Node).

Node is a server technology that interprets the JavaScript code and allows programmers to build and run their web applications from the server (the server is part of the back end of the website). With the invention of Node, programmers began creating many applications and JavaScript libraries that do not work in the browser—only from the server. Programmers also began developing JavaScript code that can be run from either the client side or the server side. Code that can be run from either side is called Isomorphic JavaScript.

With the capability Node provided, programmers began to explore new ways that JavaScript could be used outside the web. It has become an increasingly popular technology with some major companies. LinkedIn, Groupon, PayPal, and Netflix all use Node.js in their applications.

CHAPTER 4

LEARNING JAVASCRIPT

Getting started in learning JavaScript is the easy part. If you have access to a computer with a web browser that is connected to the internet, you are ready to go. Every modern web browser (like Google Chrome, Firefox, Safari, and Internet Explorer) comes with JavaScript installed.

GET STARTED—LEARNING JAVASCRIPT

When it comes to actually learning JavaScript, there are several approaches from which to choose. Many schools offer computer science classes or after-school clubs, and that would be a great starting point. These will allow a student to learn some basics of computer science while meeting other students with similar interests.

Outside of school, summer camps across the United States are dedicated to teaching kids how to code. Searching for "JavaScript camps" online is an effective way of identifying and signing up for computer programming—and specifically JavaScript—summer courses.

>> Schools can be a good place to look first for computer science classes or clubs. Though not often a part of the standard curriculum, many schools see the importance of understanding computers.

Even if the cost or time commitment of a summer camp is too much, there are online JavaScript courses that allow beginners to learn the language at their own pace. Better yet, some of these courses are free. An internet search for "JavaScript online courses" will provide an ambitious coder with a selection of online courses being offered. Alongside these online courses, there are also some online games designed to teach basic coding skills (Scratch and Code Combat are two examples) and YouTube videos that teach programming or JavaScript basics.

>>LEARN TO CODE—ONLINE RESOURCES

For students who want to get started learning the basics of computer programming, here are some online resources:

- Alice lets users create animations and simple games in 3D. Students from middle school to colleges and universities use it to learn the basics of programming. Alice is free to download at https://www.alice.org.
- Codeacademy users work at their own pace learning basic programming skills and JavaScript development.

>> For students who want to teach themselves the basics of computer programming, Scratch is just one program that can provide a good start.

Codeacademy is free to use at https://www.codecademy.com.

- Code Combat lets users learn computer science while playing a game. Users solve puzzles and defeat the enemies while learning and using JavaScript code. It is available at https://codecombat.com.
- Lightbot is a programming puzzle game in which users create visual programs to move a little robot. It is available at http://lightbot.com.
- Scratch lets users program their interactive stories, games, and animations. Students who want to can share their work with others in the Scratch online community. Scratch is free to download at https://scratch.mit.edu.

INTERNSHIPS

Another route to improving a beginner's programming skills might be an internship. Some big-name computer companies, like Apple, Microsoft, Google, and Facebook, offer internship programs for high school students. While these programs are highly competitive, there may be many local businesses that are willing to bring a teen onboard for a summer internship, especially if he or she is willing to work for free in exchange for the opportunity to work and learn alongside skilled programmers. Learning in a real-life work environment is one of the best ways to develop practical skills quickly. An internship can also go a long way toward helping a young coder decide if a computer science career is the right choice for him or her.

Even with so many programming languages out there, JavaScript is an excellent starting point. One of the main reasons for this is that JavaScript is available, literally right at everyone's fingertips. The only things needed to start writing and running JavaScript programs are a computer and a web browser. The JavaScript interpreter is built right into the web browsers so they can read the JavaScript programs.

Even if you have no interest in a programming career, countless careers today are impacted by technology in different ways. Learning a programming language is a useful skill for any young person. Steve Jobs, the cofounder of Apple Inc., said in a 1995 PBS interview, "Everybody in this country should learn how to program a computer, should learn a computer language, because it teaches you how to think." Learning a programming language also strengthens problem-solving skills.

The key is to remember that even as a student, there are many resources available to help anyone learn more about programming in general—and learning JavaScript is a great first step down the road of coding.

TURNING CODING INTO A CAREER

If you enjoy computer languages—writing code and testing it out until computer applications and software are working just right—then you might want to consider a career as a computer programmer. During your high school years, take the most advanced math classes your school offers, along with science courses, because these teach the logical thinking skills that a programmer needs. And, of course, take any computer science course available at your school.

Most programmers have earned a bachelor's degree, and it is possible to earn a master's or doctoral degree in computer science. If you are looking for a college with a programming career in mind, search for schools with strong computer science departments. The majors might be computer science, computer software engineering, computer systems analysis, information science, information technology, programming languages, or web development, depending on the school.

Typically, programmers will learn several programming languages while still in school. Some programmers specialize in one area of computer programming while others know and use several computer languages, working as generalists in their jobs. With a computer science degree, programmers are equipped to tackle new languages easily as they progress in their careers. So many programmers continue to be lifelong learners, updating their skills through continuing education courses and professional development seminars.

>>JOBS, JOBS, JOBS

For anyone who enjoys the problem-solving parts of coding or the idea of learning new computer languages, here are some computer-related careers that might be a good fit. These jobs generally require a bachelor's degree for landing an entry-level position. All salaries reflect the 2016 median pay.

(continued on the next page)

(continued from the previous page)

- Computer Programmers—$79,840 per year
  - o They write and test code for computer applications and software programs.

- Software Developers—$102,280 per year
  - o They are the creative minds behind computer programs. Some develop applications while others develop the underlying systems that run devices or control networks.

- Web Developers—$66,130 per year
  - o They design and create websites. They control the website's look, along with its technical aspects, like performance and capability.

- Information Security Analysts—$92,600 per year
  - o They develop the security measures that protect computer networks and systems.

- Database Administrators—$84,950 per year
  - o They use software to store and organize data, ensuring the data is available for users and protected from unauthorized attacks.

- Computer and Information Systems Managers—$135,800 per year
  - o They plan, coordinate, and direct an organization's computer-related activities.

Source: Bureau of Labor Statistics—*Occupational Outlook Handbook.* April 2018. https://www.bls.gov/ooh/computer-and -information-technology/computer-programmers.htm#tab-8.

PROGRAMMER—ALL IN A DAY'S WORK

In a normal day, computer programmers might find themselves busy with the following tasks:

- Writing new software programs using a variety of computer languages
- Updating existing software programs
- Testing and debugging software programs to find and fix errors in the computer code
- Creating and testing code in programming environments
- Using code libraries of basic code as they write software programs

According to the Bureau of Labor Statistics, about 38 percent of computer programmers are working for companies that do computer systems design and related work. Finance and insurance companies, software publishers, and manufacturing companies are businesses that also hire computer programmers. Since programmers can work from most any location where there is a computer and internet access, programming is a job in which many people work from home. About 5 percent of computer programmers are self-employed.

The Bureau of Labor Statistics *Occupational Outlook Handbook* suggests that these qualities are important for a person seeking a computer programmer job: analytical skills, concentration, being detail oriented, and troubleshooting skills. Learning any programming language—including JavaScript—is a great way to acquire these abilities.

CHAPTER 5

JAVASCRIPT AND THE OTHER LANGUAGES

T he names are somewhat similar—JavaScript and Java. But exactly how are the two programming languages connected? In addition, many beginner programmers have questions about which languages are the best. While there is no "best" language that is great at doing everything, each language has situations in which it is extremely good and others in which it may not be as functional.

JAVASCRIPT AND JAVA—ARE THEY COUSINS?

Both JavaScript and Java are object-oriented (OOP) languages. This means that the programmer defines not only the data type, but also the types of operations. For this reason, some programmers refer to JavaScript and Java as distant cousins.

At the time JavaScript was first released, Sun Microsystems was already selling Java. So when Netscape and Sun Microsystems prepared to release JavaScript, they thought that giving it the JavaScript name might allow the software to benefit some from the popularity that already existed for Java. Over time, there has

>> In the mid-1990s, Sun Microsystems was already selling Java. When JavaScript was created, Netscape and Sun Microsystems joined together in a licensing agreement to release the new programming language.

been some confusion, with JavaScript sometimes mistakenly thought of as just a lighter version of Java.

Here is how Brendan Eich talked about the JavaScript connection to Java, in an InfoWorld interview:

So it's 1995, the Web is very early … Java was coming along at the same time but it required you to use a high-powered programming language and then run a compiler and put your code into a package that became an applet that was part of the page but it was in a little silo. It was kind of walled off. And it was hard to do—it was for professional programmers … Whereas JavaScript was just a little snippet you could write, you could copy somebody else's, you could learn as you went. And we were pushing it as a little brother to Java, as a complementary language like Visual Basic was to C++ in Microsoft's language families at the time.

The basic difference is that Java is a programming language, while JavaScript is a scripting language (a scripting language depends on another application in order to work—that application is the browser). Programmers use Java to create stand-alone applications. They would not use JavaScript for stand-alone applications. Rather, they would run JavaScript on a browser to add interactive features to web pages.

Another difference is that Java is a compiled computer language, while JavaScript is an interpreted language. Where Java used to run on both browsers and servers, by the mid-2010s, it was used mainly on servers. By comparison, JavaScript used to run only on browsers, but now it runs on both browsers and servers. JavaScript and Java do not share the same plug-ins; they require different plug-ins. (Plug-ins are the software pieces added to an existing program to give it a new feature or capability.)

>>BOOSTING COMPUTER SCIENCE KNOWLEDGE—ONLINE COURSES

After completing a basic course through a school or other organization, many beginners want to take their learning to the next level. Many universities and companies offer excellent free (or inexpensive) online courses, with courses available in computer science topics, including JavaScript.

- edX: Harvard University and MIT founded edX, a platform for online learning. Universities like Harvard, MIT, Purdue, Berkley, UC San Diego, and companies like Microsoft produce the edX computer science courses. www.edx.org.

- Coursera: Stanford University professors founded Coursera, offering courses from a wide range of universities and companies. While some courses require a fee, there is also free content. www.coursera.org.

- Khan Academy: Khan offers students short video lessons on a wide range of topics. Lessons and practice exercises that also go along with the videos are available on the Khan website. www.khanacademy.org.

- Treehouse: Treehouse offers a wide range of coding classes for beginners and more advanced coders. There is a monthly fee for using the Treehouse courses, but a seven-day free trial lets students check it out before deciding to use it. www.teamtreehouse.com.

>> Alongside JavaScript, Python is another of the most popular programming languages in the world, according to a Stack Overflow survey in 2017.

VECTOR ICON

JAVASCRIPT AND THE WEB PROGRAMMING LANGUAGES

JavaScript is not the only web programming language. For the programmer who is interested in web development work, there are a number of web development languages that would be a good addition to a programmer's toolbox, both on the client side and the server side. After JavaScript, some of the most popular web programming languages, according to a Stack Overflow 2017 survey, include: SQL, Java, C#, Python, PHP, C++, C, and TypeScript.

JAVASCRIPT ON THE CLIENT SIDE

Web development can be separated into two pieces: the front end (client side) and the back end (server side). On the client side, HTML and CSS are basic but important pieces. While these are not programming languages, they do give the website its structure and style.

When programmers bring together JavaScript, HTML, and CSS, they can create beautiful, efficiently run web pages. However, there are some other choices in this equation. Like the JavaScript language itself, these JavaScript frameworks and libraries continue to evolve. Over time, the older frameworks and libraries lose some popularity and are replaced with newer, innovative technologies.

Here is a sampling of the libraries and frameworks available to programmers working in JavaScript. (A library is pieces of code that can be reused, typically related to a specific question or topic. A framework, simply put, is a collection of libraries.) Angular, Ember, Vue, and Backbone are all popular JavaScript frameworks. React and JQuery are popular JavaScript libraries. JQuery was the first library to tackle the issue of browser compatibility. It ensures that JavaScript runs exactly the same on all web browsers, without the need for any browser-specific code.

>>JAVASCRIPT LIBRARIES—NO CARD NEEDED

Just like school and public libraries, programming languages have libraries. At standard libraries, many people can check out different books over and over again. Similarly, in a JavaScript library, programmers find files containing existing code that can be used and reused in the current program they are writing. JavaScript libraries allow programmers to reuse existing code so that they do not have to waste their programming time writing code that already exists. These libraries help to stretch and extend JavaScript's capabilities. Programmers who write the code initially put it out into the programming world for others to use. While there are hundreds of free JavaScript libraries to choose from, React, JQuery, Lodash, and Underscore are some of the more popular libraries.

>> With the arrival of the Node.js environment in 2009, JavaScript could be run easily from the web server side.

JAVASCRIPT ON THE SERVER SIDE

Running JavaScript on the server side is not a new thing, but the idea got a huge boost in 2009 when Node.js, a server-side environment arrived on the scene—giving developers the capability to build servers and network applications with JavaScript. The end result was web servers that performed well and ran easily, programmed by anyone who already knew the familiar JavaScript language. Besides JavaScript, other web programming languages on the server side include Java, Python, Ruby, C#, PHP, Go, and Swift.

Sometimes in reading or listening to discussion about JavaScript, one common term you might hear is "vanilla JavaScript." In the same way that vanilla ice cream is a plain flavor with no added toppings or special flavors, vanilla JavaScript is just plain JavaScript, without using any of the JavaScript libraries or tools. Vanilla JavaScript is used on some popular websites like Facebook, YouTube, Twitter, Pinterest, and Netflix, to name just a few.

CHAPTER 6

JAVASCRIPT DEVELOPMENT TOOLS

J ust like mechanics have tools in their toolbox that help them perform certain specific tasks, programmers have programming tools. These programming tools might also be called software development tools. A programming tool is a software program that developers or programmers use to create, edit, or debug new software programs. These tools help programmers and developers fix bugs, write code that runs more efficiently, and guard against security risks, to name just a few advantages of the tools. In other words, tools make the development process easier for programmers.

According to Stack Overflow's 2017 developer survey, here are some (but certainly not all) of the more popular JavaScript development tools.

BUILD AND DOCUMENTATION TOOLS

As JavaScript is used for more complex projects, programmers have begun to use build tools to help them install things and do

```
154        .pipe(=-fix:  at
155         prefix: '.min'
156         suffix: '.min'
157       }) : gutil.noop())
158       .pipe( isProduction ? gulp.dest( paths.s
159       .pipe( isProduction ? gutil.noop() : brov
160                                ? gutil.noop() : bro
161   });
162
163   // JS
164   gulp.task('js', function() {
165     var scriptBase = gulp.src( basePaths.scrip
166       .pipe($.plumber({
167         errorHandler: function (err) {
168           new gutil.PluginError('JS BAS
169           this.emit('end');
170         }
171       }))
172       .pipe($.concat('ui-base.js'))
173       .pipe(isProduction ? gulp.dest( pat
174     var scriptVendorBase = gulp.src( base'
175       /* plumber({
176                            function (err)
                              r('JS
```

>> Today, with JavaScript being used for more complex projects, programmers use build tools to help make their coding work a little simpler.

things as they build web applications. Webpack, Grunt, Gulp, and Yeoman are some of the more popular JavaScript build tools.

IDEs (integrated development environments) and text editors are another tool that developers and programmers use as they build and test software. The IDEs are commonly a software suite that includes a code editor, a compiler and/or interpreter, and a debugger. The text editors are more streamlined, including just the basic features. Webstorm is a powerful and popular IDE used by programmers working on advanced JavaScript development. Atom and Brackers are some of the popular text editors.

Documentation describes how the JavaScript software works and how to use it. Some programmers describe documentation as

>>CELEBRATE THE PROGRAMMERS !

Coders have their own day, dedicated to celebrating all their hard work. Each year, International Programmers Day (or the Day of the Programmer) occurs on September 13 (except leap years, when it is celebrated on September 12). The day is celebrated on September 13 because it is the 256th day of the year—and 256 is the number of distinct values represented by an eight-bit byte. Also, 256 is the highest power of 2 that is less than 365 (the days in a year). Valentin Balt and Michael Cherviakov were the two men who first pushed for the idea of an annual day to recognize programmers. Thanks to their efforts, International Programmers Day became a reality in 2009.

the thing that turns an application from a black box into a glass box. It allows the user to see and understand how the application works. Swagger, jGrouseDoc, and Docco are examples of popular JavaScript automated documentation tools.

TESTING, DEBUGGING, AND SECURITY TOOLS

Programmers use JavaScript testing tools and testing frameworks to identify and fix bugs and errors. This testing helps programmers ensure that their software is as error free and stable

>> Errors in code can be frustrating; coders use testing and debugging tools to make sure their software is as bug free and stable as possible during the development process.

as possible before users begin using the application. Jasmine, Mocha, and PhantomJS are some of the most popular JavaScript testing tools.

When programmers are writing new computer code, it is easy for errors to show up. Those errors can sometimes be stubborn to find and fix. That is where JavaScript debugging tools come to the rescue. JavaScript Debugger, Chrome Dev Tools, and ng-inspector are some of the popular JavaScript debugging tools.

Programmers use security-testing tools to analyze the computer code they write to find any potential weaknesses that would let an attacker gain access to the computer system. Armed with the right security tools, a programmer can work to find and fix any potential security weaknesses before an attack occurs. Snyk, Node Security Project, RetireJS, and Gemnasium are examples of JavaScript security tools.

CODE OPTIMIZATION AND ANALYSIS TOOLS

Programmers look to code optimization tools and code analysis to be sure that the code they have written runs in the most efficient and effective way possible. Using these tools, a programmer can create a program that is smaller in size, faster, and uses less memory. JSLint, JSHint, and Flow are examples of these popular JavaScript tools.

Version control tools can be very helpful when a team of programmers or developers is working on a software project. The control tools allow team members to collaborate smoothly, compare files, and to track the changes from one version to the next, as they move along through the development process. Whether a team's project is small or large, these tools can help to ensure that the software development runs smoothly. Git and Subversion are examples of JavaScript version control tools.

PACKAGE AND DEPENDENCY MANAGEMENT TOOLS

Software is stored in packages. These packages contain components such as applications, collections of libraries, and services. When programmers and developers are working in teams, package and dependency management tools can help them better track and update the libraries. Bower, Yarn, and Duo are some of the popular package and dependency management tools.

Technology today continues to take giant steps forward in our ever-changing world. The programming languages are a key piece of the technology even as humans watch the products that power the world change and advance with new discoveries. Billions of people use web applications in every part of life, from work to school to shopping to social life. JavaScript is part of the foundation of those web applications. As a programming language, JavaScript has grown and evolved to keep up with changing technology like faster web browsers and large applications. Programmers rely on JavaScript for anything they are building on the web. Its relative simplicity and powerful capabilities make it an important piece of any programmer's skill set. Looking to the future, JavaScript has an important place in the technologies of both today and tomorrow.

AJAX Stands for Asynchronous JavaScript and XML. It is a time-saving technique that allows data from the server to refresh the relevant parts of a web page without having to reload the whole page.

APPLICATION Software program designed for a specific purpose; also called an app.

BACK END The server side of a computer system.

CLIENT SIDE As it relates to JavaScript, this means the computer language's commands are being carried out by the web browser.

CODE Instructions that tell the computer what to do.

COMPILED LANGUAGES Programming languages that are translated by running them through a compiler (a software program).

COMPUTER PROGRAMMING LANGUAGES Instructions for the computer written in a language that somewhat resembles English.

CSS Stands for Cascading Style Sheets, and it is a style sheet language. CSS gives website content its style by defining things like layout, colors, and fonts.

ECMA European Computer Manufacturers Association. ECMA sets standards for computer systems. ECMA-262 (or ECMAScript) is JavaScript's commercial name.

FRAMEWORKS A collection of libraries, tools, and compilers.

FRONT END The web development that happens at the web browser (not on the server), also called client side.

HTML Stands for HyperText Markup Language, and it is a markup language. HTML gives a website its structure by defining things like paragraphs, tables, headers, and embedded images.

INTERPRETED LANGUAGES Programming languages that are translated into machine language by the web browser.

JAVASCRIPT ENGINE The program that understands JavaScript code and carries out its instructions. JavaScript engines are usually found in web browsers.

LIBRARIES JavaScript code, written by a programmer, and made available to other programmers (like a library of books, borrowed and used by many people).

MACHINE CODE Computer language consisting of 1s and 0s. Also called native code or machine language.

SCRIPT A short computer program that gives instructions for tasks (that can be done one at a time if carried out by a person).

SINGLE THREADING In programming languages, it means one command is executed at a time.

SYNTAX Rules that define a programming language's structure.

TOOLS Software programs that helps programmers or developers create, edit, or debug new software programs. Can also be called software development tools or programming tools.

FOR MORE INFORMATION

Association for Computing Machinery (ACM)
2 Penn Plaza, Suite 701
New York, NY 10121-0701
(212) 869-7440
Email: acmhelp@acm.org
Website: https://www.acm.org
Facebook: @AssociationForComputingMachinery
Instagram and Twitter: @TheOfficialACM
ACM is a computing society with its goal of advancing
   computing both as a science and as a profession.

Association for Information Science and Technology (ASIS&T)
8555 16th Street, Suite 850
Silver Spring, MD 20910
(301) 495-0900
Email: asist@asist.org
Website: https://www.asist.org
Facebook and Twitter: @assist_org
ASIS&T is an association that "bridges the gap between
   information science practice and research."

Association for Women in Computing (AWC)
PO Box 2768
Oakland, CA 94602
Email: Info@awc-hq.org
Website: http://www.awc-hq.org/home.html
AWC is a professional organization for women in computing.
   Members include programmers, system analysts, operators,
   technical writers, and internet specialists.

Association of Professional Canadian Consultants
Suite 703
157 Adelaide Street West
Toronto, ON M5H 4E7
Canada
(416) 545-5213
1-800-483-0766 ext. 493
Email: tamarah@apcconline.com
Website: https://www.apcconline.com
Facebook: @APCCOnline
Twitter: @APCC_Canada
APCC is an association that supports information technology
workers who operate as independent small consulting
businesses.

Canada Information Processing Society (CIPS)
1375 Southdown Road
Unit 16 - Suite 802
Mississauga, ON L5J 2Z1
Canada
(905) 602-1370
 1-877-ASK-CIPS (275-2477)
Email: info@cips.ca
Website: http://www.cips.ca
Facebook: @CIPS.ca
Twitter: @CIPS
CIPS is Canada's association for information technology
professionals.

Computing Research Association (CRA)
1828 L Street NW, Suite 800
Washington, DC 20036-4632
(202) 234-2111
Email: info@cra.org
Website: https://cra.org
Facebook: @computingresearch
Twitter: @CRAtweets
CRA joins industry, government, and academia "to strengthen
    research and advanced education in computing."

IEEE Computer Society
2001 L Street NW, Suite 700
Washington, DC 20036-4928
(202) 371-0101
Email: help@computer.org
Website: https://www.computer.org
Facebook: @ieeecomputersociety
Twitter: @computersociety
IEEE is a membership organization focused on computer
    science and technology.

National Association of Programmers
PO Box 529
Prairieville, LA 70769
(225) 278-2290
Email: info@napusa.org
Website: http://www.napusa.org
NAP is an association for programmers, developers, and
    consultants in the computer industry.

FOR FURTHER READING

Bedell, J. M. *So, You Want to Be a Coder? The Ultimate Guide to a Career in Programming, Video Game Creation, Robotics, and More!* New York, NY: Aladdin: Hillsboro, OR: Beyond Words, 2016.

Beedie, Duncan. *Get Coding! Learn HTML, CSS, and JavaScript and Build a Website, App, and Game.* Somerville, MA: Candlewick Press, 2017.

Chinnathambi, Kirupa. *JavaScript: Absolute Beginner's Guide.* Indianapolis, IN: Que, Pearson Education, 2017.

Edelman, Brad. *Computer Programming: Learn It, Try It!* North Mankato, MN: Dabble Lab/Capstone Press, 2018.

Haverbeke, Marijin. *Eloquent JavaScript: A Modern Introduction to Programming.* San Francisco, CA: No Starch Press, 2015.

Minnick, Chris, and Eva Holland. *JavaScript For Kids For Dummies.* Hoboken, NJ: John Wiley & Sons, 2015.

Morgan, Nick, and Miran Lipovaca. *JavaScript for Kids: A Playful Introduction to Programming.* San Francisco, CA: No Starch Press, 2015.

Powell, Asher. *Cool Careers Without College for People Who Love Coding.* New York, NY: Rosen Publishing, 2018.

Sabatino, Michael. *Understanding Coding with JavaScript.* New York, NY: PowerKids Press, 2018.

Towaha, Syed Omar Faruk. *JavaScript Projects for Kids.* Birmingham, UK: Packt Publishing, 2016.

Aranda, Michael. "What's the difference between JavaScript and ECMAScript?" Free Code Camp, October 28, 2017. https://medium.freecodecamp.org whats-the-difference-between-javascript-and-ecmascript -cba48c73a2b5.

Bort, Julie. "The geeky reasons why September 12 is International Programmer's Day." Business Insider, September 12, 2016. http://www.businessinsider.com why-september-12-is-international-programmers -day-2016-9.

Bureau of Labor Statistics. *Occupational Outlook Handbook.* "Computer Programmers." Retrieved February 1, 2018. https://www.bls.gov/ooh/computer-and-information -technology/computer-programmers.htm#tab-1.

Choudhary, Nidhi. "Infographic: Top 6 Benefits of Node.js for Application Development." To The New, August 24, 2017. http://www.tothenew.com/blog /top-6-benefits-of-node-js-for-application-development.

DA-14. "The Ultimate List of JavaScript Tools." June 1, 2017. https://da-14.com/blog/ultimate-list-javascript-tools.

Grantham, Nick. "9 Sites that Make Programming for Kids Fun." Fractus Learning, November 16, 2017. https://www .fractuslearning.com/2011/12/14/programming-for-kids.

Jones, Darren. *JavaScript: Novice to Ninja.* Melbourne, Australia: SitePoint, 2017.

Kolowich, Lindsay. "Web Design 101: How HTML, CSS, and JavaScript Work." HubSpot, July 28, 2017. https://blog .hubspot.com/marketing/web-design-html-css-javascript.

Krill, Paul. "JavaScript creator ponders past, future." InfoWorld, June 23, 2008. https://www.infoworld.com /article/2653798/application-development/javascript -creator-ponders-past--future.html.

Morgan, Nick. "Javascript for Kids." http://pepa.holla.cz /wp-content/uploads/2015/11/JavaScript-for-Kids.pdf.

Mozilla MDN Web Docs. "Introduction." November 29, 2017. https://developer.mozilla.org/en-US/docs/Web/JavaScript /Guide/Introduction.

Mozilla MDN Web Docs. "What is JavaScript?" October 23, 2017. https://developer.mozilla.org/en-US/docs/Learn /JavaScript/First_steps/What_is_JavaScript.

Netscape Company Press Relations. "Industry Leaders to Advance Standardization of Netscape's JavaScript at Standards Body Meeting." November 5, 1996. https://web .archive.org/web/19981203070212/http://cgi.netscape .com/newsref/pr/newsrelease289.html.

O'Grady, Stephen. "The RedMonk Programming Language Rankings: January 2017." RedMonk.com, March 17, 2107. http://redmonk.com/sogrady/2017/03/17 /language-rankings-1-17.

Peyrott, Sebastian. "A Brief History of JavaScript." January 16, 2017. https://auth0.com/blog/a-brief-history-of-javascript.

Prinsloo, Kyle. "13 Best Programming Languages to Learn in 2017." Usersnap. Retrieved February 15, 2018. https:// usersnap.com/blog/programming-languages-2017.

Ramel, David. "JavaScript Dominates 2017 Stack Overflow Developer Survey." ADT Mag, March 22, 2017. https:// adtmag.com/articles/2017/03/22/stack-overflow-survey .aspx.

Rosoff, Matt. "The Most Interesting Things Steve Jobs Said In a "Lost" Interview Showing Next Week." Business Insider, November 11, 2011. http://www.businessinsider.com the-best-quotes-from-the-lost-steve-jobs-interview-showing -this-weekend-2011-11.

Shiotsu, Yoshitaka. "Web Development 101: Top Web Development Languages to Learn in 2018." Upwork.com, November 28, 2017. https://www.upwork.com /blog/2017/11/top-web-development-languages-2018.

Techopedia staff. "The Pioneers of Computer Programming." July 4, 2013. https://www.techopedia.com/2/27836 /development/programming-tools /the-pioneers-of-computer-programming.

Techopedia—The IT Education Site. "Programming Tool." Retrieved January 5, 2018. https://www.techopedia.com /definition/8996/programming-tool.

Wayner, Peter. "JavaScript vs. other languages: Live long and prosper?" Tech Beacon. Retrieved February 13, 2018. https://techbeacon.com/javascript-vs-other-languages.

w3schools.com. "HTML Styles—CSS." Retrieved February 11, 2018. https://www.w3schools.com/html/html_css.asp.

INDEX

ABOUT THE AUTHOR

Donna B. McKinney is a writer who lives in North Carolina. She spent many years writing about science and technology topics, like chemistry, space science, and robotics, at the US Naval Research Laboratory in Washington, DC. Now she enjoys writing about science and technology for children and young adults. She is also a contributing writer for *Diversity in Action* magazine, where she writes about STEM careers.

PHOTO CREDITS

Cover Kdonmuang/Shutterstock.com; cover, back cover, pp. 1, 4–5 (background) © iStockphoto.com/letoakin; p. 5 Rawpixel.com/Shutterstock.com; p. 8 Stephen VanHorn /Shutterstock.com; p. 9 The Photo Works/Science Source /Getty Images; p. 11 © iStockphoto.com/temizyurek; p. 14 An147yus/Shutterstock.com; p. 16 © AP Images; p. 17 360b/Alamy Stock Photo; p. 20 Catrina Genovese/WireImage /Getty Images; p. 22 Denis Golov/Alamy Stock Vector; p. 25 JuliusKielaitis/Shutterstock.com; p. 26 Tal Revivo/Alamy Stock Vector; p. 28 Getty Images; p. 33 Arthur Tilley/Stockbyte /Getty Images; p. 34 Phil's Mommy/Shutterstock.com; p. 41 James Leynse/Corbis Historical/Getty Images; p. 44 Tim Evseev /Shutterstock.com; p. 46 GaleanoStock/Shutterstock.com; p. 48 Thongchai Kitiyanantawong/Shutterstock.com; p. 50 ESB Professional/Shutterstock.com.

Design and Layout: Nicole Russo-Duca; Editor: Siyavush Saidian; Photo Researcher: Karen Huang